HEADLINES OF WORLD WAR I

Patience Coster

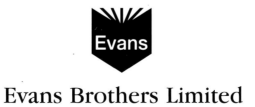

Evans Brothers Limited

Contents

Pictures on page 4 show Captain Scott,
Book illustration, The *Titanic*,
George V and Queen Mary

Pictures on page 5 show Italian infantryman,
Tsar Nicholas II, Vladimir Ilyich Lenin,
Emmeline Pankhurst, signing the Armistice

Introduction

World War I, the Great War, began in 1914 and ended in 1918. It marked the end of an old way of life in Europe. At the start of the twentieth century, wealthy landowners formed an upper class that kept up a high standard of living. They employed armies of servants to run their huge houses. These aristocrats sent their sons to private schools (called public schools in Britain). Here they were taught a strict code of behaviour. They were to become their countries' leaders. They believed it was right to die for the honour of one's family and one's country.

These young men became the officers on both sides in the war. They led their men 'over the top' of the trenches, and were often the first to die. The men they commanded had joined up with enormous enthusiasm. They, too, believed in their country, right or wrong. On both sides, they suffered appalling hardships. Millions died in the mud of France and Belgium and on the Russian (Eastern) front. Those who survived the horrors of World War I no longer believed in the notion of war as 'glorious'. They returned home believing that, from now on, things would be different.

As the dust of war began to settle, people started to question whether it had been worth fighting and why it had been fought at all. The immediate cause of World War I had been the assassination of an Austrian leader in the Balkans. But how had this regional event sparked a vast international conflict? Largely to blame were the old alliances and rivalries between European nations. These had become fragile and dangerous. Following the events in Sarajevo in June 1914, European states had tumbled one by one into a catastrophic and bloody war, like a house of cards falling.

In the USA, nobody wanted to go to war. But when the German U-boats continued to sink their ships, the USA joined the Allies. The USA survived World War I with her lands intact and her economy in good shape. In Europe and in the East, the survivors faced poverty and even starvation. Their towns and cities were in ruins. Men were clamouring for work, women were demanding voting rights, and a new struggle for personal equality was beginning. In Germany, Italy and Russia, leaders who promised a better world were certain of a following.

1910

BUDGET ROW

February 14, London, England In the British Parliament a row is raging between the House of Commons and the House of Lords. Last year the Lords refused to agree the Liberal government's budget. The mainly Conservative Lords tend to vote against Prime Minister Asquith's government, which is not very strong.

KING DIES SUDDENLY

May 6, London, England King Edward VII has died. Now there will be no quick solution to this government's problems. Mr Asquith had asked the King to allow 200 Liberals to be made peers (lords). Only the monarch may create peers. The King was considering this request when he fell ill.

ELECTION NEWS

December 20, London The Liberals' success in the general election means that steps may be taken to reform Parliament.

CRIPPEN SENTENCED

October 22, London, England Dr Hawley Crippen's trial for murder ended today. The jury heard how he poisoned his wife in January. He hid her body in his cellar and disappeared with his secretary, Ethel Le Neve. In July, Mrs Crippen's body was found. Dr Crippen and Miss Le Neve were discovered on board a ship bound for Canada. Crippen has been found guilty. He will be hanged next month.

Dr Crippen (with moustache) and Miss Le Neve leave the SS *Montrose* under arrest.

German and British royalty attend the funeral of King Edward VII.

FUNERAL OF EDWARD VII

May 21, Windsor Castle, England Seven European monarchs attended the funeral of King Edward VII. The late King's cousin, Kaiser Wilhelm II, accompanied the Queen.

US PRESIDENT IS HOME

June 19, New York, USA Former US president Theodore Roosevelt returned home today after spending ten months hunting in British East Africa.

President Roosevelt (left, in hat) enjoys a picnic with his family.

ASSASSINATION ATTEMPT

June 15, Sarajevo, Bosnia-Herzegovina An attempt has been made on the life of the Governor of Bosnia, General Varesanin, during the state opening of parliament. A Serb student named Bogdan Zerajic fired five shots at the governor, but failed to kill him. Zerajic then shot himself. The dead student is said to be a member of the Black Hand, a group that wants Bosnia-Herzegovina to leave the Austrian Empire.

FAMILY MEETING

November 4, Potsdam, Germany Tsar Nicholas of Russia is visiting Potsdam for a meeting with his cousin, Kaiser Wilhelm of Germany. The monarchs are discussing political issues concerning Russia and Germany. Following Austria's annexation of Bosnia-Herzegovina in 1908, the Tsar has been pleased to receive the Kaiser's assurance that Germany will not support Austrian ambitions in the Balkans.

NEWS IN BRIEF...

YOUNGSTERS PREPARE FOR ADVENTURE

February 6, New York Be prepared to meet America's first Boy Scouts! A group of boys met today to form a troop like those in Britain. American girls will be able to join a troop – the Camp Fire Girls.

A FASHION SENSATION

September, London, England Fashionable women's skirts are now so tight at the ankle that walking is almost impossible. The Pope is shocked by the new fashion and has publicly condemned it.

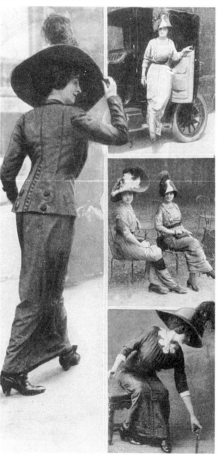

Reduced to a 'Chinese toddle' in hobble skirts.

PORTUGAL LOSES ITS KING

October 5, Lisbon, Portugal During the past hundred years, Portugal has been very unstable. Today there was a coup against King Manoel. After bloody fighting in the capital, the king fled to Gibraltar. The army and navy, who led the coup, have proclaimed Portugal a republic.

HEAVENLY BODY

May 20, London, England Halley's comet, which visits our skies every 75 years, can be seen on clear nights. Comets are feared by some people as a bad omen.

1911

July 2	German gunboat sent to Morocco
August 17	Strikes cause havoc in Britain
November 1	War between Italy and Turkey

THE SPIRIT OF UNREST

STRIKING AND RIOTS IN BRITAIN

August 17, London, England About 200,000 British railway workers have come out on strike. Dockers at all the main ports have been on strike for two months. Shops are running short of food supplies. There is no coal or electricity in some towns and people have been rioting. The Home Secretary, Winston Churchill, has sent 50,000 troops to stop the riots. Armed soldiers are guarding railway stations and signal boxes. All over Europe, agricultural and industrial workers are striking and rioting for better pay and conditions. Governments may need to provide some social benefits for workers.

Troops and police arrive with armoured vehicles to confront strikers in Liverpool, England.

HEATWAVE BRINGS TRAGEDY

August 30, London, England For once, the British weather has been too good. On August 8, the temperature soared to 36.7°C. More than 2,000 children have died in the heatwave.

INSURANCE FOR ALL

December 16, London, England The government has announced that all low-paid workers in Britain are to receive health insurance. Now they can visit the doctor for free. Employers are complaining that they cannot afford to pay into this scheme, and many are cutting back on staff.

ENGLISH ROYAL EVENTS

THE KING IS CROWNED

June 22, London, England Today King George V and Queen Mary were crowned in Westminster Abbey. The Abbey was completely full. The congregation included lords, archbishops, members of parliament and representatives of the Empire. Motion picture cameras filmed the scene outside the Abbey, but they were not allowed inside.

The view from Buckingham Palace as the royal coach leaves for Westminster Abbey for King George V's coronation.

CELEBRATIONS IN INDIA

December 12, Delhi, India Britain's King George V has been crowned Emperor of India before a huge crowd. The splendidly dressed princes of India were in attendance.

King George V and Queen Mary in Delhi.

GERMAN TROOPS LAND IN MOROCCO

July 2, Agadir, Morocco Yesterday the Germans sent a gunboat, *Panther*, to the port of Agadir. Morocco has been under French protection since 1906, and Germany's action has alarmed France. Britain is concerned that Germany may establish a naval base at Agadir. With its large army, Germany is very powerful and the French and British are worried that it may be a threat to world peace. If Britain and France ally themselves against Germany, it is likely that war could follow. Talks between the three countries are planned soon. Meanwhile the Austrians and the British are building up their navies.

ITALY ATTACKS LIBYA

November 1, Tripoli, Libya Italian marines have landed at Tripoli. Italy has also bombed towns and shelled ports in Libya. Turkey controls Libya, but the Turks have been neglecting their once-powerful empire, which includes countries in the Balkans. These countries may seize the chance to rebel against Turkey while her empire is weak.

CHINA IS REBORN

December 29, Peking, China The Chinese people have ended the Manchu dynasty. The first president of the new Chinese republic intends to modernise China. He has forbidden men to wear pigtails, a hairstyle introduced by the first emperor of the Manchu dynasty in the 1600s.

A citizen of the new China has his pigtail removed.

NEWS IN BRIEF...

POPULATION INCREASE

April 8, London, England The British population has increased by almost 11 per cent in ten years. France's population has not changed. Russia's has increased by a third, to 160 million. In recent years the USA has welcomed thousands of immigrants. Many of them are from Eastern Europe and have emigrated to the USA in search of work. The US population has risen from 76 to 92 million.

ATOMIC THEORY

May, Manchester, England The British physicist Ernest Rutherford has published a scientific paper about atomic theory. In it he describes an atom as a small, heavy nucleus surrounded by electrons. Scientists believe Rutherford's discovery will be of great significance as research continues in this field.

CURIE WINS AWARD

December 10, Paris, France Marie Curie has been awarded her second Nobel Prize. Mme Curie has extracted pure radium from a rock called pitchblende.

WHAT THE FASHIONABLE SET IS WEARING

Autumn, London, England Dressmakers and milliners have done good business in this Coronation year. Hats are very tall and topped with feathers. Skirts are long and straight. Blouses have a V-shaped neckline. Gentlemen are equally handsomely dressed. They go to the City in tail coats, striped trousers and top hats. In the country they may wear tweed jackets and plus-fours.

1912

March	Bulgaria and Serbia sign alliance treaty
July 1	Morocco given to the French
July 22	Concerns over strength of British fleet
October 18	Italy wins Libya from Turkey
November 30	War starts in the Balkans

HOME RULE FOR IRELAND

May 2, London, England The British government wants Ireland to have its own parliament and run its own affairs. The Liberal government has introduced a Home Rule Bill. Many Protestants living in northern Ireland (Ulster) do not want Home Rule.

ULSTER UNIONISTS SIGN COVENANT

October 5, Belfast, Northern Ireland Two hundred Ulster Unionists, members of a party that opposes Home Rule in Ireland, have signed a Covenant saying they will not recognise a Home Rule parliament. More than 237,000 men and 234,000 women have added their names to the Covenant.

SECRET TREATY

March The Balkan states of Bulgaria and Serbia have signed an alliance with each other. It is thought that Russian diplomats have been secretly involved in bringing the two rival states together.

GERMANY WITHDRAWS

July 1, Fez, Morocco By a treaty signed in Fez, France will in future control Morocco. The German Navy has been asked to leave. In exchange for their withdrawal from Agadir, the Germans will be given 154,000 sq km of French territory in the Congo.

The Ulster Covenant opposes a Home Rule parliament in Ireland.

Ulster's Solemn League and Covenant.

Being convinced in our consciences that Home Rule would be disastrous to the material well-being of Ulster as well as of the whole of Ireland, subversive of our civil and religious freedom, destructive of our citizenship and perilous to the unity of the Empire, we, whose names are under-written, men of Ulster, loyal subjects of His Gracious Majesty King George V., humbly relying on the God whom our fathers in days of stress and trial confidently trusted, do hereby pledge ourselves in solemn Covenant throughout this our time of threatened calamity to stand by one another in defending for ourselves and our children our cherished position of equal citizen-ship in the United Kingdom and in using all means which may be found necessary to defeat the present conspiracy to set up a Home Rule Parliament in Ireland. ¶ And in the event of such a Parliament being forced upon us we further solemnly and mutually pledge ourselves to refuse to recognise its authority. ¶ In sure confidence that God will defend the right we hereto subscribe our names. ¶ And further, we individually declare that we have not already signed this Covenant.

The above was signed by me at................................ "Ulster Day," Saturday, 28th September, 1912.

—— God Save the King. ——

WOMEN WANT THE VOTE

March 1, London, England Today a group of women smashed almost all the shop windows in three of London's smartest streets. They are suffragettes, who demand that women should be allowed to vote for MPs. Their leader, Emmeline Pankhurst, smashed the windows of No. 10 Downing Street, the prime minister's residence. Mrs Pankhurst has been arrested (right).

WAR FLARES IN BALKANS

November 30, Sofia, Bulgaria Romania, Serbia, Montenegro, Bulgaria and Greece have formed the 'Balkan League'. The League is fighting Turkey and its dwindling empire. It has pushed the Turks out of European Turkey, apart from the area around Constantinople. Turkey has governed these provinces very badly and the Turkish government is weak and inefficient. The Great Powers are concerned that the Balkan League will gain too much land influence. For the first time, aircraft are being used to watch over troop movements in the battle zone.

TITANIC SINKS

April 14, New York, USA The ocean liner *Titanic* has hit an iceberg on her first voyage across the Atlantic. There were not enough lifeboats for all the passengers, and more than 1,580 people are feared drowned.

Passengers escape in lifeboats from the sinking *Titanic*. A survivor said that the ship turned gradually on her nose, 'like a duck that goes for a dive.'

AMERICAN INDIAN IS OLYMPIC HERO

July 22, Stockholm, Sweden A record number of competitors have taken part in the Olympic Games. This year's hero is an American Indian named Jim Thorpe (below). He won both the pentathlon (five events) and the decathlon (ten events).

The opening ceremony of the Olympic Games.

ITALIANS REMAIN IN LIBYA

October 18, Tripoli, Libya According to the Treaty of Lausanne, signed today, Italy's occupation of Libya is legal. Turkey is defeated. The Turks are sending their troops to the Balkan provinces, where they are fighting a losing battle with the Balkan League. The Great Powers are anxious to ensure that this war does not spread beyond the Balkans.

NEWS IN BRIEF...

NEW US PRESIDENT

November 5, Washington DC, USA The Democratic Party has won the US presidential election. Woodrow Wilson succeeds William Taft as president. Wilson said the country needs 'New Freedom' in politics and a strong government.

NAVY TO MODERNISE

July 22, London, England The First Lord of the Admiralty, Winston Churchill, has asked the government for money to improve the fleet. He wants all warships' engines to run on oil rather than coal. Mr Churchill is alarmed at the growing strength of the German Navy.

DEFENCE AGREEMENT

July As a consequence of the crisis in Morocco, Britain and France have made an agreement. It states that, in the event of a major war in Europe, the British fleet will guard the North Sea and the English channel. The French fleet will guard the Mediterranean Sea.

1913

TROUBLE IN THE BALKANS

YOUNG TURKS DISMISS TREATY

January 23, Constantinople, Turkey The Turkish government has been overthrown by a political party called the Young Turks. Its members object to a treaty that was signed last month with the Balkan League. The treaty stated that Turkey should give up her lands in Europe.

NEW TREATY ENDS WAR

May 30, London, England Diplomats from the major European powers have today signed a treaty to end the Balkan War. Austria is concerned that Serbia, a member of the Balkan League, is becoming too powerful. A new state, Albania, is to be created. This will prevent Serbia gaining a coastline on the Adriatic Sea. Serbia has been given lands in Macedonia as compensation.

WAR STARTS AGAIN

June 29, London, England Bulgaria has invaded Serbia, in a declaration of war. The Greek army is advancing on Serbian positions in the south. Romania and Turkey are concerned that Bulgaria is becoming too strong. Their armies are also advancing on Bulgarian positions. Who knows how this state of affairs will end?

SUFFRAGETTE KILLED AT RACES

June 14, London, England Thousands of women have attended the funeral of suffragette Emily Davison. She died when she threw herself in front of the King's horse at Epsom races.

GOVERNMENT PLAYS CAT AND MOUSE

March 31, London, England By a new Act of Parliament, suffragettes on hunger strike in prison will be temporarily released. The suffragettes call this the 'Cat and Mouse Act': the cat lets the mouse go, then pounces on it again.

BRAVE EXPLORERS HONOURED

February 14, London, England A memorial service has been held at St Paul's Cathedral for Captain Scott and his companions who died in the Antarctic. Last week a search party found their bodies. They were in a snow-covered tent 17 km (11 miles) from their supply base. The men had died because they had been too weak to reach their supplies.

Captain Scott and his team at the South Pole.

BALKANS HAVE NEW BOUNDARIES

August 10, Bucharest, Romania According to a peace treaty signed today, the Balkan countries have agreed how to divide the lands. Serbia, Romania and Greece have all gained territory, but Bulgaria has gained little. The Balkan Wars nearly resulted in a wider European conflict. The British Foreign Secretary has said, "We are sitting on gunpowder."

BULGARIA DEFEATED

July 31, Bulgaria Serbia has defeated Bulgaria in a decisive battle. Tsar Nicholas of Russia has been trying to agree a peace deal between the two countries, without success. Russia is angry with Bulgaria for going to war.

RUSSO-GERMAN CRISIS

November, Constantinople, Turkey Russia is angry that a German officer, Otto Liman von Sanders, has been sent to train the Turkish army. Russia suspects that Germany may want to extend its influence in Turkey.

DRIVE ENDS IN TRAGEDY

April 20, Paris, France Two children and their governess have drowned in a tragic accident. The car they were driving in plunged into a river. The children's mother is the famous dancer, Isadora Duncan.

NEWS IN BRIEF...

NO TO CHANNEL TUNNEL

August 5, London, England The British government no longer plans to build a tunnel beneath the English Channel. The government is afraid that it would make England easy to invade.

BALKAN TREATY SIGNED

September 29, Constantinople, Turkey Bulgaria and Turkey today signed a peace treaty with each other. Both countries have been severely weakened by the recent Balkan Wars. There is a growing sense of concern among other European countries about the extent of German influence in Turkey and Bulgaria.

WHICH IS THE NUDE?

March 30, Chicago, USA Artist Marcel Duchamp has caused a stir with his painting entitled *Nude Descending a Staircase*.

SKYSCRAPER CITY

April 24, New York, USA At 422 m (1,384 ft) high, the new Woolworth building is the tallest in the world.

IRELAND IS ON EDGE

December 4, London, England The situation in Ireland is tense. The Home Rule Bill was passed by the House of Commons in January, but the Lords rejected it. They sympathise with the Ulster Unionists.

ZEPPELIN DISASTER

October 17, Berlin, Germany The world's largest airship, the Zeppelin *L2*, has exploded in the worst disaster of its kind to date. Twenty-seven passengers have been killed.

1914

MARCHING TO WAR

ARCHDUKE IS SHOT DEAD

June 28, Sarajevo, Bosnia-Herzegovina The Austrian Archduke Franz Ferdinand and his wife have been shot dead. They were visiting the Balkan province of Bosnia-Herzegovina, part of the Austrian Empire. The killer is a Serbian student named Gavrilo Princip.

Archduke Franz Ferdinand and the Duchess Sophie shortly before their assassination.

SERBIA BLAMED FOR MURDER

August 4, London, England The murder in Sarajevo has started a great war. The Austrians are blaming the Serbian government for planning it. Austria has declared war on Serbia, and on Russia because it supports Serbia. France supports Russia. Germany has sided with Austria and declared war on Russia and France. German troops have invaded Belgium. Britain has a treaty with Belgium and has declared war on Germany.

Soldiers are being recruited at offices all over Britain. This one is in Trafalgar Square, London.

THE BEF LEAVES FOR FRANCE

August 7, Southampton, England Crowds lined the streets today to watch the British Expeditionary Force (BEF) leave for France.

BOTH ARMIES MARCH SOUTH

September 2, France After fierce fighting at Mons in Belgium, the BEF has withdrawn to the south. The men have had very little rest or food, and their new boots are causing blistered and swollen feet. They have marched 320 km (200 miles) in 13 days. The Royal Flying Corps is watching from the air as the Germans march towards Paris.

BATTLE OF THE MARNE

October 14, Ypres, Flanders German soldiers have been recalled to defend their eastern boundary from Russian attack. The remaining troops have been driven back across the Marne River. They have suffered heavy casualties. The Allied armies have now marched north to Ypres in Flanders. They are digging trenches for protection on the flat plain. The Germans cannot now take Paris, but are trying to reach the port of Calais.

TRENCH WARFARE

November 11, Ypres, Flanders One side shells its opponent's trenches, then their soldiers advance. The survivors in the trench fire on the advancing soldiers. Shells and rifle-fire cause enormous numbers of casualties. Both sides are exhausted.

GERMANY COUNTS HER LOSSES

November 15, Ypres, Flanders From a German report: 'We have 134,000 dead and wounded. Most of them are very young men, straight from school or university.'

BRITISH WIN FALKLANDS BATTLE

December 11, London, England The Royal Navy is celebrating the sinking of four German battleships today. The German Navy was trying to capture the Falkland Islands, which are British owned. But two British battleships surprised them and attacked, with guns blazing.

German and British soldiers meet on friendly terms on Christmas Day.

CHRISTMAS TRUCE

December 25, Ypres, Flanders Today has been one of goodwill, with no guns fired. Men from both sides walked into 'no man's land' and talked and smoked together. The fighting will start again tomorrow.

THE EASTERN FRONT

GERMAN VICTORY OVER RUSSIA

August 30, Tannenburg, East Prussia The Russians have two armies in East Prussia. They contain many young recruits and they are not as well trained as the German troops. The Germans outmanoeuvred the Russians at the Battle of Tannenburg. The Germans, led by General von Hindenburg, took 120,000 prisoners. The Russian advance has been halted.

NEWS IN BRIEF...

BIG BERTHA

August 15, Liege, Belgium The Germans have developed a huge mobile gun. It is known as 'Big Bertha' and is named after the wife of its inventor, Gustav Krupp! The gun is being used to shell Allied troop positions in Liege.

CLOSE TO PARIS

September 5, France The German army is so close to Paris that soldiers can see the Eiffel Tower in the distance.

RUSSIANS BATTLE FOR POLAND

November 25, Poland The Russians are fighting to keep the German army out of Poland. Four days ago they had the Germans surrounded. Suddenly the Germans cut through the Russian lines, taking 16,000 prisoners.

CASUALTIES OF WAR

November More than 80,000 British soldiers have been wounded or killed in the past three months. The French casualties are 50,000. In Britain more than one million men have volunteered for the army.

CARS ARE BIG BUSINESS

January 5, Detroit, USA Henry Ford's car factory is doubling workers' wages to a minimum of $5 a day.

Mr Ford's cars are no longer built one at a time. The parts are put together on an assembly line.

1915

January 1	Turks blockade Russia at the Dardanelles
April 22	Poison gas used at Ypres
April 25	Allies land at Gallipoli
May 8	Germans sink *Lusitania*
October 12	Edith Cavell executed
December 21	Serbia defeated by Germany and Bulgaria
December 31	Defeated Allies leave Gallipoli

THE GALLIPOLI CAMPAIGN

DARDANELLES CLOSED TO SHIPPING

January 1, London, England Russia is cut off from her allies. Turkey will not allow any Russian ships through the Dardanelles, Russia's main route to the Mediterranean and Aegean seas.

DISASTER IN DARDANELLES

March 19, London, England A fleet of Allied battleships has tried to sail through the Dardanelles. The Turks fired on the fleet from both sides of the peninsula. A French battleship exploded and two British battleships hit mines and were sunk.

SOLDIERS FACE GAS HORROR

April 22, Ypres, Flanders The Germans are using a new weapon, poison gas, which burns the eyes, throat and lungs. Stretcher bearers are carrying victims to the Red Cross tents behind the lines.

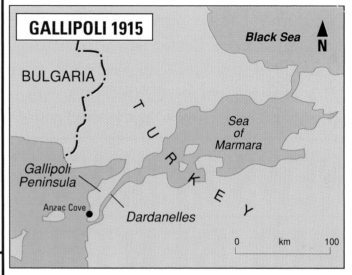

ALLIES LAND AT GALLIPOLI

April 25, London, England Under Turkish fire, the Allies have landed men on the Gallipoli peninsula at the entrance to the Dardanelles. Hundreds of men have been killed. Hospital ships have taken the wounded to Egypt. The soldiers climbed huge cliffs under fire, then dug trenches for cover. There are too few men left to carry out a proper attack. The troops are from many different countries, including Britain, France, Australia and New Zealand.

The Landing by George Lambert (right) shows Anzac troops scaling cliffs at the Dardanelles.

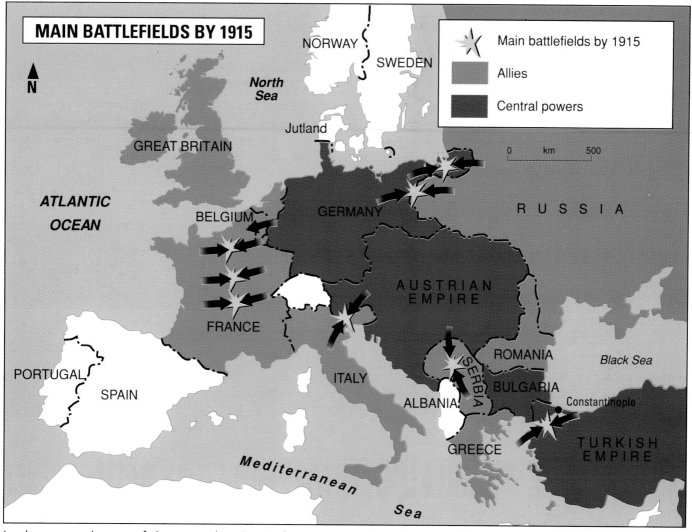

MAIN BATTLEFIELDS BY 1915

N

NORWAY
SWEDEN
North Sea
Jutland
GREAT BRITAIN
ATLANTIC OCEAN
BELGIUM
GERMANY
R U S S I A
FRANCE
AUSTRIAN EMPIRE
ROMANIA
Black Sea
PORTUGAL
SPAIN
ITALY
SERBIA
BULGARIA
ALBANIA
Constantinople
GREECE
TURKISH EMPIRE
Mediterranean Sea

Main battlefields by 1915
Allies
Central powers

0   km   500

In the second year of the war, the Central Powers are fighting the Allies on five major fronts.

French soldiers in their trenches.

Turkish guns at Gallipoli.

British troop positions at Anzac Cove.

NO ADVANCE AT GALLIPOLI

June 25, London, England The Allies have landed more troops at Gallipoli. The weather is very hot, many men have died of dysentry, and the fighting goes on day and night. The Turks are determined not to surrender the peninsula. If they did, the Allies could take the capital, Constantinople.

TORPEDO SINKS BRITISH LINER

May 8, London, England A German U-boat has torpedoed the British passenger ship, the *Lusitania*. More than 100 Americans were among the 1,200 people who drowned. U-boats have sunk hundreds of merchant ships. The Germans are trying to stop food reaching Britain.

TROOPS LEAVE GALLIPOLI

December 31, London, England The Germans are sending troops to help the Turks. The Allies cannot hope to win; their soldiers are boarding troop ships. The retreat will go on into the New Year. The campaign has left 30,000 dead and 74,000 wounded.

GERMAN PLANS REVEALED

July 24, New York, USA Although the USA and Germany are not at war, German secret agents are spying in America. A US secret service man has uncovered German plans to wreck US ships and factories. Two German officials have been asked to leave the USA.

NURSE SHOT IN BELGIUM

October 12, Brussels, Belgium Miss Edith Cavell, a British nurse, was shot by the Germans this morning. The Germans discovered that she had helped British soldiers to escape.

SERBIA IS DEFEATED

December 21, Serbia The Germans now occupy Poland. The Bulgarians have joined the war on Germany's side and captured Serbia. The Serbs are fleeing.

The Germans executed Edith Cavell for treason.

NEWS IN BRIEF...

GERMAN PLANE BROUGHT DOWN

April 1, France A German aircraft has been shot down by a French plane using an ingenious invention. The pilot, Roland Garros, has developed a way of firing a machine gun through the propeller of his aircraft. He added steel plates to the propeller blades, to divert the bullets. Up until now, pilots have relied on taking 'pot-shots' at one another with a revolver or rifle.

NAVAL ATTACK

January The German First High Fleet has bombarded the British coastal towns of Hartlepool, Whitby and Scarborough. The naval attack has left eighteen civilians dead.

ZEPPELIN RAID

May 31, London, England A bombing raid on London by German Zeppelin airships has left 28 people dead and 60 injured. The British government fears there could be further raids in the months to come.

POET DIES AT SEA

April 23, Greece Rupert Brooke, the British poet, died today of blood poisoning. He was 27 years old. Brooke (below) was an officer on a ship sailing for the Dardanelles. He will be buried on the Greek island of Skyros.

1916

February 13	Women enrol in war jobs
May 31	Battle of Jutland
June 5	Lord Kitchener drowns at sea
June 24	French withstand German siege at Verdun
July 1	Record casualties on the Somme
September 15	Russian success with the Brusilov offensive

THE WAR AT SEA

U-BOATS SINK NEUTRAL SHIPS

April 18, Washington DC, USA German U-boats continue to sink the ships of countries that are not at war. Some of these are US ships. Last year Germany apologised to the USA for the sinking of the *Lusitania*.

WARSHIPS FIGHT FIERCEST BATTLE

June 1, London, England A bloody battle involving 259 warships and 100,000 men has been fought in the North Sea off Jutland. British and German fleets bombarded each other with shells, torpedoes and guns. Many ships were sunk and hundreds of sailors killed.

WOMEN DO WAR WORK

February 13, London 400,000 women have joined a new Land Army. 80,000 women have joined the Voluntary Aid Detachment (VAD), working in hospitals and driving ambulances.

NEWS FROM THE BATTLEFIELDS

'THEY SHALL NOT PASS,' SAY FRENCH

June 24, Verdun, France The Germans have bombarded French troops with more than two million shells. They want to capture the steel-and-concrete fortresses that ring the town of Verdun. The casualties are appalling.

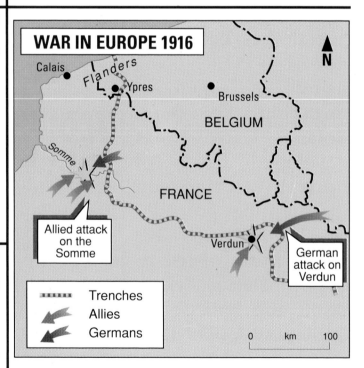

A map showing the major battles of 1916, fought between enemy trenches in Belgium and France.

WAR MINISTER IS DEAD

June 5, London, England The British Secretary for War, Lord Kitchener, has perished at sea. He was sailing to Russia to talk with the Tsar about new battle plans when his cruiser hit a mine and sank. Lord Kitchener's recruiting poster is well known to British people.

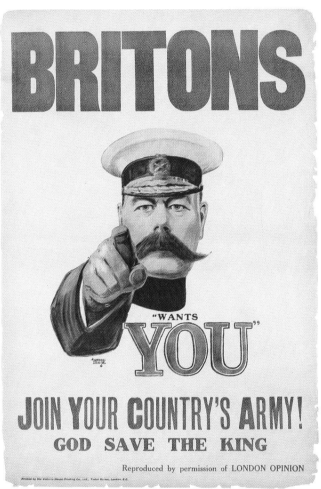

BRITISH ADVANCE IN TANKS

September 15, France Today, 18 British armoured tanks crossed the boggy craters and fallen trees of no man's land. From close range they fired on German positions. The crews report that the tanks are dreadfully noisy and stiflingly hot, but that they may change the way the war is fought.

PORTUGAL ENTERS WAR

February, Lisbon Germany has formally declared war on Portugal. This is because the Portuguese government has ordered its navy to seize German ships in its harbours.

SOMME CASUALTIES

July 1, France The British have bombarded the Germans on a front 28 km (17 miles) long to relieve pressure on the French at Verdun. Nearly two million men have died at Verdun and on the Somme.

EASTER RISING

May 12, Dublin, Ireland Troops have had to be recalled from France and Belgium to go to Ireland. Two weeks ago, 1,000 Irish nationalists proclaimed an Irish Republic. After a fierce battle, British troops restored order.

Explorer Ernest Shackleton in arctic gear.

GREAT EXPLORER IS RESCUED

August 30, London, England Two years ago, Ernest Shackleton set out with a team of explorers to cross Antarctica. The team's ship became trapped in pack-ice and drifted for nine months. At last the explorers escaped to a remote island. A relief expedition has now picked up all the men.

SURPRISE ATTACK SUCCEEDS

September 15, Eastern Front On June 4, the Austrian Archduke's birthday party was interrupted by a surprise Russian attack. The Russians advanced on the Austrian army and now occupy 100 km (62 miles) of enemy territory. The attack was co-ordinated by Commander Alexei Brusilov.

ELECTIONS IN US AND BRITAIN

December 7, Washington DC, USA Last month Woodrow Wilson was re-elected president of the USA. In Britain, the new prime minister, David Lloyd George, is determined to bring the war to a speedy finish.

The four allied leaders. Woodrow Wilson is on the right.

A VIEW FROM THE TRENCHES

France "If only the people of England could have seen what I saw yesterday they would not grumble about air raids. I saw motor lorries sunk in the mud over the wheels, also horses with just part of their heads showing above the swamp....
There are men now in the trenches full of water who are nearly dead, they are fast dying of cold, they go sick, see the doctor, go back and try to stick it until they get relieved..."

(Soldier Daniel Sweeney from *Greater Love*, ed. M. Moynihan, W. H. Allen, 1980)

US TROOPS ENTER MEXICO

June 21, Mexico US troops have entered Mexico in search of a rebel named Pancho Villa (centre, below). He has led raids across the border into North America. The Americans are taking tough action to protect their citizens. They fear that war may break out between the USA and Mexico.

NEWS IN BRIEF...

SERBS SALUTE EXTRAORDINARY WOMAN

November 30, Belgrade, Serbia Flora Sandes was nursing in Serbia when the Serbian army fled into Albania last December. She dressed as a man and joined the army. She was seriously wounded fighting the Turks. The Serbs have given her a bravery medal.

VICTORIA CROSS FOR YOUNG HERO

July 6, London, England Royal Navy sailor Jack Cornwall has been posthumously awarded the VC. He died six weeks ago at the Battle of Jutland. He was only 16 years of age.

VERDUN RECOVERY

December 18, Verdun, France The French army has retaken the forts of Douaumont and Vaux, capturing 11,000 prisoners.

MOVIES MAKE MONEY

October 31, Hollywood, USA Hollywood film stars like Mary Pickford (below) now earn up to a million dollars per year.

1917

REVOLUTION IN RUSSIA

TSAR DEPOSED BY GENERALS

March 15, Petrograd, Russia Russian army generals have told Tsar Nicholas II that he must give up his throne. The Tsar is in charge of the army. The Russian people are sick of the war and blame him for the deaths of two million men in battle. They have asked the government to make peace with Germany. Meanwhile, starving people are rioting all over the country and factory workers are on strike.

BOLSHEVIKS' BID FOR POWER

October 26, Petrograd, Russia The leader of the Bolshevik Party, Vladimir Lenin, wants to replace the weak government. Lenin's Red Guards seized the Winter Palace, the Russian seat of government, today. The Guards locked the government ministers in a cellar. Lenin is now ready to form a new socialist government.

GERMAN TELEGRAM TO MEXICO

March 1, London, England The British government has intercepted a telegram from Germany promising support for Mexico if war should break out between Germany and the USA.

RUSSIA BOWS OUT OF WAR

December 5, Brest-Litovsk, Poland The new Bolshevik government in Russia has signed an armistice with Germany and the other Central Powers. For the Russians, the war is over.

A portrait of the Bolshevik leader, Vladimir Lenin.

ALLIES FACE HINDENBURG LINE

March 30, Flanders From a German report: "Our armies have been digging fortified trenches behind the front line, from Arras to Soissons. This Hindenburg Line is about 50 km (31 miles) long.... In front are many fences of barbed wire. No Allied troops will be able to cross it."

AMERICA ENTERS THE WAR

April 6, Washington DC, USA President Wilson's government has declared war on the Germans. The president said: "The world must be made safe for democracy."

THE AGONY OF WAR

August 30, France One of the worst battles of the war is being fought near the village of Passchendaele. It is raining all the time, and soldiers fight ankle deep in mud. Wounded men drown in shell-holes. The hail of shells and bullets never stops.

YANKS JOIN UP IN THEIR MILLIONS

June 5, Washington DC, USA Recruiting offices opened for twelve hours today to cope with demand. Nearly ten million men have responded to posters like the one below and joined the US army.

ITALIAN DEFEAT

November 9, Italy The Italians have been fighting the Austrians in northeast Italy with some success. Today, however, they were defeated at Caporetto. They have lost a huge area of land, and thousands of men to the German and Austrian armies.

PLANES BOMB LONDON

June 14, London, England German planes launched a bombing raid on London yesterday. One bomb hit a school, killing many children.

TURKISH ARMY RETREATS

December 9, Jerusalem Allied forces have taken Jerusalem, and the Turks are in retreat. Commander of the British forces is General Edmund Allenby.

ENGLAND FACES FOOD SHORTAGES

March 20, London There is only about one month's supply of wheat left in Britain, and there are shortages of other foods too. These have been caused by U-boats sinking British merchant ships.

WOMEN URGED TO JOIN NAVY

November 29, London, England The Admiralty wants to recruit women into the Navy. The women will be part of the newly formed Women's Royal Naval Service (WRNS).

NEWS IN BRIEF...

RED CROSS IS HONOURED

December 10, Stockholm, Sweden This year's Nobel Peace Prize has been awarded to the International Red Cross. Red Cross volunteers are working in appalling conditions on the battle fronts.

BEF REMEMBERED

August 25, London, England A new decoration, the Mons Star, will be given to all those members of the BEF who fought at Mons and Ypres in 1914.

GREEK KING DEPOSED

June 29, Greece Greece has entered the war on the side of the Allies. The pro-German king has been deposed.

KING CHANGES NAME

July 17, London, England King George V has changed the name of the royal house to Windsor. The name was originally Saxe-Coburg-Gotha. The British king has abandoned all his family's German titles. He does not feel that such connections are acceptable now Britain is at war with Germany.

BIRTH CONTROL ROW

September 30, New York Margaret Sanger has been sent to prison for opening a birth control clinic in the USA.

Mrs Margaret Sanger, pioneer of birth control.

1918

April 10	German troops advance from Hindenburg Line
August 8	Allies push Germans back
October 3	Arabs and Allenby take Damascus from Turks
November 4	Wilfred Owen dies
November 11	Armistice is signed
December 14	Lloyd George wins British general election

GERMANS LAUNCH ATTACK

April 10, France Germany's peace treaty with Russia has enabled her to move troops from the Eastern to the Western Front. A week ago, a million German soldiers advanced from the Hindenburg Line towards the River Marne. They bombarded the Allied trenches for five hours. The Allied army is retreating.

Woodrow Wilson has been re-elected as president of the USA. Americans support his decision to enter the war in support of the Allies.

GERMAN ACE PILOT KILLED

April 21, France The Red Baron has been shot down and killed by ground fire. This German airman was famous for flying his distinctive red plane with great skill and courage. He was responsible for shooting down 80 Allied aircraft.

Manfred von Richthofen – the Red Baron.

ALLIES SUDDENLY GAIN GROUND

August 8, Amiens, France Away from the Hindenburg Line, the German troops are not well protected. The Allies are attacking German gun positions and bombing their trenches. US soldiers are pouring into Europe. Hundreds of Germans are surrendering every day.

The French and British armies advance near Amiens.

TURKS ARE OUT OF THE WAR

October 3, Damascus The Turks are defeated. The Allies control Damascus. Arab troops led by Emir Feisal and an Englishman, Lt. Col. T. E. Lawrence, have driven the Turks out of Arabia. They have also arrived at Damascus. The Turks have offered a reward of £20,000 for Lawrence.

A painting of T. E. Lawrence, the Englishman who led attacks on many Turkish troop trains.

RUSSIAN ROYAL FAMILY MURDERED

July 16, Siberia The deposed Tsar of Russia, his wife, daughters and son were shot dead today by members of the Russian security police.

Tsar Nicholas II with his only son, Alexis.

AIRCRAFT IMPROVING ALL THE TIME

April 1, London, England The Royal Flying Corps has been renamed the Royal Air Force (RAF). In 1914, Britain had only 272 aircraft, and the engines were made abroad. Today there are more than 22,000 planes, with British-made engines.

WAR IS OVER AT LAST

November 11, Forest of Compiegne, France At 11 a.m. today, four years of continuous fighting ended. The Allies and the Germans signed an armistice agreeing a ceasefire. The guns are silent at last. The German Kaiser has abdicated and fled to Holland. Germany is now a republic.

Allied and German leaders, pictured here after signing the armistice that ended World War I. The agreement was signed in a railway carriage.

War graves on what was the Western Front, near Arras in France. One of the tasks facing Europe following the war is to erect lasting memorials to the millions of fallen soldiers.

LLOYD GEORGE WINS ELECTION

December 14, London, England David Lloyd George's Coalition Party has won the general election and has 459 seats in Parliament. The prime minister told voters he wanted to make Britain "a land fit for heroes to live in". The main task of the new government will be to give jobs to soldiers returning from the war and to restore the economy.

ANTI-WAR POET DIES IN FRANCE

November 4, France The British poet, Wilfred Owen, has been killed in action in France. He was 25 years old. Many young men have been taught that death in battle is a valiant and noble end. In one of his poems, Owen called this kind of teaching 'the old lie'. His poetry reflects war's stupidity and waste. Owen died just as the war was ending.

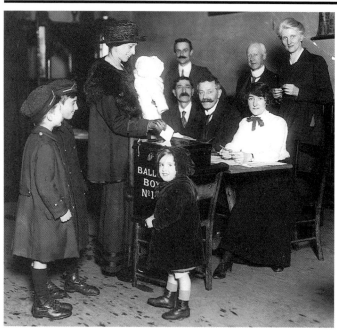

WOMEN GAIN THE VOTE

December 28, London, England Women over the age of 30 have been allowed to vote for the first time in a general election. Suffragettes still want the voting age for women to be 21, as it is for men.

This woman, voting for the first time, has brought her young family with her.

BITTER END

November 11, France An entry from a US army sergeant's diary reads: "Runner in at 10.30 with order to cease firing at 11 a.m. ... 306th Machine-Gun Company on my right lost twelve men at 10.55, when a high explosive landed in their position. At 11.00 sharp the shelling ceased on both sides ... we don't know what to say."

NEWS IN BRIEF...

MUSIC BAN

November 30, New York, USA During the time that the USA has been at war, the New York Symphony Orchestra has refused to play music by living German composers.

SECRET ARMY?

November, France Around 200,000 African-American soldiers have served in the US army. Black US soldiers are segregated (separated) from white US soldiers. Most of the black soldiers have fought alongside the French army.

1919

January 12	Paris Peace Conference opens
May 7	Huge war reparations demanded of Germany
June 21	German sailors scuttle ships at Scapa Flow
June 28	Treaty of Versailles signed

PEACE PROPOSALS

USA SUGGESTS COUNCIL TO PREVENT WAR

February 14, Paris, France About three-quarters of the world's population is represented by leaders of 32 states at the Paris Peace Conference. The delegates are working out a treaty which they hope will avoid war in the future. The US president, Woodrow Wilson, has suggested that there should be a council to preserve the peace. It is likely to be called the 'League of Nations'.

GERMANY MUST PAY

May 7, Paris, France The Treaty of Versailles has finally been agreed. President Wilson wants Europeans to forget the war and start afresh. But there is much bitterness in Europe. The treaty states that Germany started the war and says she must pay 'reparations' of about £6,600 million to the Allies.

GERMANS APPALLED BY TREATY

May 31, Paris, France The German Chancellor refuses to sign the peace treaty, and has resigned. The Germans are horrified by the amount they must pay in reparations.

FLEET SUNK AT SCAPA FLOW

June 21, Scotland German prisoners of war have sunk 70 of their own ships moored at a British naval base off the north coast of Scotland. The German admiral said that he was ordered never to surrender his warships.

German sailors arrive on shore after scuttling (sinking) their ship at the naval base, Scapa Flow.

SILENT SIGNING OF TREATY

June 28, Paris, France Today two German representatives arrived at the Palace of Versailles. They entered the Hall of Mirrors, where the presidents of the USA and France, and the prime ministers of Britain and Italy sat in silence. The Germans signed the peace treaty and left without saying a word. The Treaty of Versailles has placed severe restrictions on Germany. It states that her army must be limited to 100,000 men, with no tanks, no heavy artillery and no poison-gas supplies.

The German delegation (carrying papers) at Versailles.

EXTREMISM TAKES ROOT

January 15, Berlin Communists Rosa Luxembourg and Karl Liebnecht have been murdered. They led a group called the Sparticists, who tried to start a revolution. Germany is in chaos, and political parties with extreme views are springing up.

POLAND WINS INDEPENDENCE

June 28, Warsaw, Poland The Treaty of Versailles has granted Poland independence. Poland has also been given a strip of land crossing German territory, which allows her access to the Baltic Sea.

PROTEST IN CHINA

November 4, Peking The peace treaty has given Japan part of Shantung Province in China. This was once German territory. The decision has been accepted by the Chinese government, but 3,000 students have protested against it in Tiananmen Square.

In March 1919, this wireless telephone was used to transmit signals from Ireland to Nova Scotia.

ITALIAN HERO HOLDS FIUME

September 23, Italy The military leader Gabriele D'Annunzio has occupied Fiume in Yugoslavia with 2,000 men. D'Annunzio has popular support, but not the Italian government's approval.

FASCISTS GAIN SUPPORT

October 31, Milan, Italy A journalist named Benito Mussolini has founded a new political party called the Fascists. After only seven months, it has a membership of 17,000.

NEWS IN BRIEF...

DIFFERENT THOUGHTS ON THE WAR

Autumn, France Georges Clemenceau said: "The terrible responsibility which lies at her [Germany's] doors can be seen in the fact that not less than seven million dead lie buried in Europe, while more than twenty million others carry upon them the evidence of wounds and sufferings..."

Captain E. N. Bennett of Britain said: "The fundamental falsehood on which the Versailles Treaty is built is the theory that Germany was solely and entirely responsible for the war. No fair-minded student of the war and its causes can accept this..."

FIRST WOMAN MP

December 1, London, England Today Lady Nancy Astor took her seat in the House of Commons. She has been elected as MP for Plymouth.

Lady Nancy Astor, MP.

NEW REPUBLICS

December 30 Since 1910, the former monarchies of Portugal, China, Russia, Austria and Germany have decided to elect leaders instead.

RELATIVITY IS RIGHT

March 29, London, England The Royal Society of London has confirmed that the Theory of Relativity, formulated by physicist Albert Einstein, is correct.

Albert Einstein, the physicist.

PEOPLE OF WORLD WAR I

David Lloyd George, British politician 1863-1945

Lloyd George entered Parliament as Liberal MP for Caernarvon, North Wales in 1890. From 1908 to 1915 he was chancellor of the exchequer. He was made minister of munitions (military equipment) in 1915, and became prime minister in 1916. Lloyd George was from a poor background and fought for social reform, such as health and unemployment benefits. He was an energetic war leader and attended the Paris Peace Conference.

Jan Christiaan Smuts, South African leader 1870-1950

During World War I, Smuts' forces attacked German colonies in East Africa. In 1917 he became a member of the Allied War Cabinet. He helped to create the RAF.

Vladimir Ilyich Lenin , Russian leader 1870-1924

Lenin was the leader of the Bolshevik Party in Russia. Following the 1917 revolution, Lenin ordered an armistice between Russia and the Central Powers. He organised a major part of the communist transformation of Russia, seizing land, businesses and property and placing them under government control.

Woodrow Wilson, US politician 1856-1924

Wilson was elected US president in 1912 and held this position until 1920. He tried to keep the USA out of World War I. But in 1917, when German U-boats continued to attack US ships, he finally asked the Senate to declare war. In 1919 Wilson was a leading figure at the post-war Paris Peace Conference, and proposed the idea of the League of Nations. He was awarded the 1919 Nobel Peace Prize.

Kaiser Wilhelm II, German emperor 1859-1941

Son of the Emperor Frederick and of a daughter of Queen Victoria. His strong character, national pride and personal vanity led other European leaders to regard him as warlike. The Kaiser took Germany to war in 1914, but he was forced to abdicate in 1918.

Erich von Ludendorff, German general, 1865-1937

General von Ludendorff took part in the first march into Belgium in 1914. He was transferred to the Eastern Front where he defeated General Samsonov at the Battle of Tannenburg. His military strategies brought about the defeat of the Serbians, and of the Italians at Caporetto. In 1918 Ludendorff planned the last great German offensive. When it failed, he asked the Kaiser to make peace. In October that year, he resigned his post and fled to Sweden.

Emmeline Pankhurst, suffragette 1858-1928

Mrs Pankhurst (maiden name, Goulden) was born in Manchester, England, and led the British suffragettes in their struggle to obtain voting rights. She was arrested and imprisoned several times for staging violent protests. During World War I she helped persuade women to go into industry and the armed services. Towards the end of her life, Mrs Pankhurst stood as a Conservative candidate for Parliament.

GLOSSARY

abdicate to give up power

Allies In World War I, the Allies were Russia, France, Britain, Belgium and Serbia. They were later joined by 18 other states, including Japan and the USA.

annexation the taking over of territory, usually by conquest or military occupation

Anzac Australian or New Zealand soldier

armistice agreement to stop a war

Balkans the mountainous region of south-eastern Europe, between Hungary and Greece

Bolshevik Party Russian political party and original Communist Party

capitalism an economic system based upon private ownership of business and trade

Central Powers In World War I, the Central Powers were Germany, Austria and Turkey

communist a follower of communism, a political movement that states a country's wealth and government should be controlled by the people for the benefit of the people

coup seizure of power, usually by the armed forces, that results in a change of government

covenant a contract or agreement

delegate a representative at a conference or business meeting

dynasty a family of rulers

dysentry an infection of the gut

Fascist a supporter of the Italian political movement founded by Benito Mussolini. Fascists encouraged military strength and national pride and were anti-communist.

fundamental basic

Great Powers Before the outbreak of World War I, the five main powers were Russia, Austria, Germany, Britain and France

physicist an expert in physics, the branch of science concerned with the properties of matter and energy

posthumous after death

radium a radioactive metal

reparations financial compensation for war damage

republic a government headed by an elected president rather than a king or emperor born to be a ruler

Sparticists a political group, formed in Germany in 1916. In 1919 it became the German Communist Party.

suffragettes women who campaigned for the vote (suffrage)

INDEX